T0294280

Wine
Dark

Wine
Dark

Poems
Jenny Drai

Black
Lawrence
Press

www.blacklawrence.com

Executive Editor: Diane Goettel
Book and cover design: Amy Freels
Cover art: "Monolith" by Valyntina Grenier

Published 2016 by Black Lawrence Press.
Printed in the United States.

Lines from "Nachtstrahl" reprinted with permission of Random House Germany.
Paul Celan, Mohn und Gedächtnis
Copyright 1952, Deutsche Verlags-Anstalt, München, in der Verlagsgruppe Random
House GmbH

for my friends and family

CONTENTS

WINE DARK

I split
where you
recited.

Blue feeble blue pink—
into a parable the

light was
tuneless.

Dark sea, the allele.
Dark ocean, the

chance but
then again comes
the book of
forty waves.

SCHEHERAZADE

When I
wove the fist
of the cloth. When I rose
out of the night
like a swarm
of sweating
verbs. I wore this
sheath across my
body as a veil.
You could see
underneath—
I was nude. Thin
flesh gauze
of the skin.
You asked for
the crimson
diaspora of capillaries
always to be
ready.

YOU HAVE AN OPINION TO MAKE DWELLING EASY

Today is for
lace. For the
daily boiling
of water.
Windows winnow
the light, help
the story
of sight. I
bend all
the self corners.

DER ABFLUG*

I felt the

clock tear.

I took a picture

of the last day.

To get here

I rode blue paper

weightless

blood for flight

to get here.

It felt like

tearing or clocks

chiming. The

waves were

marvelous. *Erstaunliche*

Wellen. And then I

ate scalloped

lettuce, inveighed

the Duke and paid

the Duke of

gambling in his

---

* the departure

7

city all the

veins it took to leave

this place in numbers.

THE DERIVATION OF 'OUTSIDE OF THINGS'

Sitting on

an oceanic

throne.

Wondering

if one's *own*

self is the story

of truth. Engrave

the lych-gate.

Upon these stones.

At no one's

behest, a world

awaits you.

ENOUGH, I SAY, RELYING ON MARROW, LYMPH, BONE

I suffer the urge to squelch
all broken
things. A dark
mouth soars.

The mouth is
catastrophe's flower.
The gaping ovens,
the white room.

I want to be good—
to say, 'these are not shards
but whole glistening
pieces.' Then
I could whittle *den Sarg aus dem*
leichtesten Holz.

A mouth of bitter iron filings.
A month on the outskirts, the window
boxes packed with dirt, purple

deliverance, violet petunias, white-yellow-green
daffodils.

To understand, I borrow
the newest alphabet. I do not understand.

Genocide has a cadence.
The track suits of modern refugees.

Dachau is a stone
park of memory, the memory
of work and death,
death and work.

Celan, the teenager
who read you on the stoop—
to you *I send a coffin*
of the lightest wood. Later, selling Duty
Free cigarettes,
UN troops in the Munich
airport, their uniforms marked
SFOR,* peace, don't
shoot, I am a youth of the thousandth
order.

---

* Indicates 'Stabilization Force,' marking on UN troops in Kosovo conflict

Paul, who murders
the river's remembrance.

Who tried, and failed,
to excise Antschel.

The differing hair
of the young
men, but all the tattered
color of a long
front line.

The world is a strange singer.
I sing before strangers.

I LIE TO YOU WHEN I SLEEP BECAUSE I AM NOT SLEEPING

I could

not pin an

orbit on

any sour cherub.

Chance is a

perfume

of bones. All I wanted

was for you to be *careless I rode*

through a path of beach

trees, thinking of watercress for the miniature

sandwiches. We witness

collapse, swarm

up through the bushes, hard red

manzanita, scale

ladders, filter *what is happening* from *what is not.*

Where I am is ambrosia to a soldier of

sleep. You rest here, beside

me, like a warm cat.

Intricacy wanes.

A low float.

Eventually, even I will

dream of poppies.

FOOD WILL BREAK YOUR AMPLIFIED HEART

Ruby,
but not stones.

I start to have longer
ideas.

The sea
escapes us, a pavonine
cavity. How
nature glances, restarts, depletes,
etcetera, ignores.
I do not
understand the zones
of this country.

Everyone
Abyss.

To say it with coldness, this
unavailable warmth.

Eyes are slits for new
faces. I couldn't decide where to
stick. An azure
bone reads to us the tar
of our life. Did
you think we all weren't delicious?

(All this wreckage, as if
at the oceanic core.)

Bon appetit, the
pure
hummus is delicious.
Enough, I
report to the flattery
of Fleet Street.

All my laces break open on sweets.
What happens to a man is a man's
word and his prospects. What
happens to a woman is a woman's word, her
prospects, what occurs to a
child, little

Ibrahim, small Hussein, *what's his name,*
this isn't a game, there is
no red ball.

A HUMAN SAYING INTO THE SCENE TO ADMONISH SILENCE

I haven't disregarded
any oblique signage.

The hatch of the boat shines
bare, framed by varnished

wood. The man
was dying,

but in another state, a different
race to shy away from

finish, the finite body
finite as a stain.

Preparing to tack, watching
the tell-tales. I will

notice his lips sewn
together with thread.

That comes later. Now is light
like a voice, some subtle

bell. Now is wind
like saffron.

During the war, his ship
had been shelled.

He swam a long mile to the
rest of his life.

Now is shifting the helm, hauling
in on the line, now

winding the winch handles,
cleating off line.

Soon he
will not

breathe again. Well, that
is the pink half of the

morning. To whom
I will announce

myself, from whom
I shall retreat.

A gull in a poem
breaks its wings

against a wicker cage.
Loss in all five senses.

Now is taking the helm, every
time like some first epoch at sea.

I grow into the wind's
bone, the current's

bending spine.
I let myself

seep through my jacket.
An impossible duration.

Sea lions bark, made of chances.
I will hear his voice, the

last time, as a sixth sense
rising out of a silence.

Then a peeling toll, a weary
traveler will sleep.

But now is glowing
sunset. Now are

notes flowing out of the pen,
once again in the dock. Now as

the antithesis of what
will come, whole

notions casting shields above
one much-abbreviated future.

And now the heavy
chest opens the

probable door,
intending

equilibrium. One heart,
lashing the white sail.

The evening, also
pink, velvety.

Like the dearest sail cover
ever sewn, this old man's

book, his life. Tomorrow the wind
will rise high in the canvas.

He moves towards his dark,
nutritive harbor.

BUT SHE WAS PURPLE CALLA LILY, MAGNOLIA IN BLOOM

Here is gold for you, to char
arrays of hidden lances.

I swear I
will paint your
night the right
hue.

Perhaps a finicky
child would
fear bears, tigers, water,
treatise.

When the alto of her voice—

first she adjourns the meeting of all
wet eyes, as she is
of finest, lacquered blonde—

breaks
over the answer, I get sticky with longing
for a different outline.

(A person

comprises the outlines

of absence.)

I cannot be always written in stone.

The first wound tastes of sorrel.

MIGHT BE LOVELY, MIGHT BE TREACHEROUS

The question had
been high
and steep. Inter-
related to a
dream
of flux. The perpetuity of the sea at work, the orphan
of salt. Here
there are
answers and
the privilege
of answers,
and sudden
rain, lash
cold. Every-
thing for a reason.
We may be dry
in this deluge.

SCHEHERAZADE

I cut into

the second night.

Pungent orange rind.

To find the pith,

the membrane

holding everything

together. Still, I have

not grown used to the scimitar's

gleam.

Love is a treasure, it

commands us to

be true. My

hands,

my feet, are my own *true.*

JANE EYRE

The story is
red like a heart.
I broke against
the current
season with six
strong lights.
Chance holds you
or breaks you.
Your light
came on
intermittently.
I walked ramparts like B.,
trailing a burning
white dress.

JANE EYRE

A lot of voices
inside me.
A lot of lengths,
phrases of all turns,
sizes like yarn
bits and
string coiled in
wooly, fuzzy
skeins. Be
my wicker basket.
Be two
hands held high
as fleece is
drawn within
a new,
precarious
boundary. Be every-
one and every-
thing, every
method of
era and
dwelling. Explain

dormancy, a sensitive
air the fingers
bear within the
problem's
heat. Break
the book's
spine, the exoskeleton
of the book.
Be kind. Bear
good will, even to Aunt
Reed. A lamp
flares.
Glaring light.
What happens to
power in a
central body?
As if I
held shawls
to my face,
the attic
of the mind.

SCHEHERAZADE

I am the
imperishable
dawn's
gold light streaking
face. Am the
illuminative
fingers falling
over that cloth, the
skin, like fair
silver hair.
Nothing is inevitable.
A vizier's gentle
daughter, un-
spoilt by
history, might
grow into
her dotage. May
temper hatred, tend
raw wounds.
Calling up
planetary
shift, the earth

three years upon an axis,

nightly stories,

ground up

flame. I am lion-

born. World-

freer. No one gets me.

No one may

keep my violet-

white teeth. I write

out vowels on my

arms and dimpled

legs. Don't say

'lithe.' I am a new type.

I am the aureate, the

unshaken, the elaborate

as unnecessary.

HELOISE, WHO SOON WILL HAVE NO INK

Disasters
are the feet
of the nine
human
souls.

The skin soul
wears gold rings, the
mouth soul, ivory
rows.

To lose a child, to lose Astrolabe.*
All the fists clench at once, including
the stomach fist.

(To bear a light in a cave, now,
that's nonsense.)

The demon soul swallows
chalky pills to forget—

---

* The son of Heloise and Abelard.

although forgetting proves
impossible.

I am cadence, a
grace, periwinkle
rain, the rust
of the dead
robin the cat drags
to your feet.
Yowls the archer
soul.

A child makes you vulnerable,
agrees the milk soul.

And who had
brightened at the
supple
knowledge offered up
on the tin plate of
the tongue, the
sixth soul, which
does not bear
a separate term? As knowledges are

catastrophes, new spaces, names

for what was heretofore

unknown.

Armfuls of

tea rose and yarrow.

Sandwiches of cucumber, hewn

off their crusts. Difficult, but

important, to remain

welcoming and

polite.

Here, in the

solarium, where the

last three souls

confine themselves to the

deities of even,

albeit complex equations.

Thus the math

soul tabulates all

possible

outcomes, tallies

parenthetical

sets.

The unseen
soul, the love soul,
writes a joke
about results. You can test me, the
love soul says. I will be here.
You will feel me like a
pinprick in the
blue middle night. I won't
let you sleep.

Astrolabe and his kite, now, that
is the ninth soul.

The kite the
child plays with
never
damages the
wind.

The air mutters.
The sea spins out its quest of salt.
A fire burns in the forest.
Women dye flax fibers for linen.
The offices are rung—
matins, lauds, compline.

Years later, shoes are polished at the
station as a man awaits the train.
Departure is always the first step to arrival.
As waves crash over the bow of a boat.
Sun runs on the water, leaves
paw prints. Decent
men and women everywhere stir
the morning porridge.
A phone rings in the future.
A lamp shines very brightly.
But here there is only a dripping, beeswax
taper. The light is warm
but sallow. Deliver me O Lord from the
tedium of this cloister.
Relieve me of loneliness, of the ecclesiastical
calendar. Find all my
souls and brand them to my
body in a surgical
operation of precision and mercy.
Up to now, I have kept
them for safekeeping in this
idle stone jar.

BATHORY

The oddest
thing I've ever
done is to
pull black gauze
across my face.
Pretending
to be Elizabeth
of Bathory.
But before the
wine-dark
blood, before
the virgin,
frozen in ice, just
when she was
a soft girl,
learning.

HOUSEHOLD FIRES

First we burn the formal dresses, then a
boa of pale white feathers.

Sulfur, somewhere.

Canute, the Viking king of England
rises out of the carpet—

he places his throne in the sea
but cannot stop the tide.

Five texts
exhumed by
human
breath.

Three platters of hard and nutty cheese.

(Insisting, at parties, that all
children fly in dreams.)

Someone is coming,
possibly
in a chariot.

Also,
the wolves
that raised us
whelp another
litter.

I am divested, the first
sign of smoke.
Refreshed by cookery.
The blue list is short.

BE YOUR OWN BLUE SWAGGER, LOVE FULL MOONS

The distortion of history
is the key of it.

His closed fist, that was years ago.
How the evil queen ate the dripping red heart.

It is necessary to become
frightened in the wilding forest.

All of us, here, landing
brand new stances.

I love you in my hair.

TABULA RASA

We may be
bones or we may
wear our bones.

If you are
lost aft or fore.

The stucco of
our lives. You sail
out of the
kitchen
this week.
Come what may, I wish
you to land safely.

Log of bones at sea.
Woke in cold,
unfamiliar
space, could not
stretch about.
Or rather only in
very small fashion.

A field of suns
burns at night.

The ocean inside us
contravenes daily.

THE WORLD COULD DRAIN YOU OR EMBOLDEN YOU

A great hold
takes over. *Thou*
art a lovely
minor entity
at the shore
of obsidian, the darker
sea glass. Pretty
are pieces. I
don't have
a soul, but still then
what explains it?
No one is
ever going to be
the blue ocean.
Thou art a lovely
sea bird, whether
gull or pelican,
cormorant
or duck.
Stand here. Just try it.

PUSH IT ALL THE WAY FORWARD

Bruised my throat
just thinking—
about *it*.
Choking on
the bone of fish.
Go. Stand in line
at the church,
bricks the
color of peaches.
The feast
day of Saint
Blaise.*
Be the greedy
placement for a
necklace of
crossed candles.
To be protected,
sworn off.
What is

---

* Saint Blaise is the patron saint of choking victims. On his feast day, candles
are crossed and laid upon the throats of churchgoers.

this spiral? What the
elaborate heat?

If you believe
in Blaise, Blaise
will come
again to you even after years
of the most silent bream.
But. You do not
go to the building, do not
attend service.
The wax tubular
columns never touch the
apex of your neck.
As a youngster, you brushed after Mass
the gilt Lamb, painted on the Tabernacle.
And then somewhere, you began
to doubt.

Let the child
see the lamb, she
has a book
about Jenny. In the Golden

Book, the lamb is a
pet and given
a bath. All the white
suds resemble
a second, pleasant
skin of fleece.
What we accomplish
when we save a
life. What
we endeavor to
destroy by accomplishing.
Never believe me
when I tell
you I am apostate.

FIRST LINES

1.

It was a dark and stormy inference of being.

2.

All happy families, you know, well, mine wasn't happy.

3.

Some years ago I noticed how many
false things I had accepted as true in my childhood...
[insert name here]
but continued to believe, and this is the
heart of religion.

4.

It is a truth universally
acknowledged that pearls have
moiré surfaces, cats
possess claws and teeth, and
gerbils eat their squiggly,
pink babies. The difficulty of the pearls
may be attributed to cost.

5.

MY GRANDFATHER VERUS / Character and self-control /
my separate godmother / unknown to me, she rode
a silver steed into the sun / *my father George* / quiet and owlish /
my ancestor Romans / who gorged on figs and olives, who
did up dormice in a savory style / *the eye of*
this storm / I could care less about his eyes, I would
care so much it hurts.

6.

In the beginning was the Word and the
Word was with Jenny, and the Word was Jenny.

7.

Who that cares much to know the history of man
ought not to forget the history of women.

8.

(As for Ralph Ellison's invisible man…)
You only see him when he wears a hoodie.

9.

He held up a forefinger of warning.
(Although this line comes neither first nor last, it nonetheless

anchors a text so massive that the water stain barely
dents it, hardly tarnishes the page.)

10.

Collectively speaking, every shard has a mouth.

All of you are lessons.

A PLACE OF ANNOUNCEMENT AND REPRIEVE

Somewhere I
sense I
am who I
imagine. An
undertaker of waves.
A thief and an
innkeeper,
all in
one indistinguishable
body. Perhaps
you think
the night at
least is canny
but even darkness is not
shrewd enough
to tell us
what isn't.
The night
only has a book
of every possible
name. Novalis
sings hymns

to it. A
blue
distance
prevails.

TODAY I AIRED AND VACUUMED THE CUSHIONS

The marrow
of an epic
is fodder for
bones. Not
really strong
fantastic
epic bones but
just regular
you or I
bones. A story
spelling a
distracted story.
A tale to rid
the tea shack
of mites. Begin
the song of
the green
soap. We are
going to
wash.

THROWN ABOUT, KNOCKED AROUND

I said I stood
in the opening
of a force
to the body.
Do it now. Let
loose dozens
of your wishes.

WITH EYES THE COLOR OF NUTMEG AND SAFETY

Here there is a metaphor solution and an actual
storm. I could have pried out another

scenario but didn't. To be alive in a

    gale,

which needs to be
    dusted. To

prepare the chicken
dinner, mildly, as previously, as if

in any other kitchen. *You chop vegetables.*

The chicken is tangential
    not because of direction or actual
amount of heat—

you seasoning the meat—

but because of fierce pulses, hair scooped

all over a face, a hat blown
off, just one moment.

And one wooden
slat pried away from the hatch.
I can see the olive

trees on the shore who castigate the wind.
We try with our anchor.
We hold ourselves to marks.

These *aren't* some kitchen stairs here.
Night in the ruin-boat, which

heels. *To*-and-fro.
To-and-*fro*.

FOLDING PAPER INTO MONEY

I'm a
good girl.
A good girl
rises early
out of her bones
to complete
a novel scene.

SCHEHERAZADE

Please, I will
be good again. You
break into the
threshold but won't
partake of the
hummus plate, the
vegetable crudités.
The story of the
self is the narrative of
the self burrowing.
I have to say
all the right
words.

SCHEHERAZADE

The lark
of danger.
Broadly
narrow.
You can
write me a
ticket if you
don't like
a cozy shell in a
globular atmosphere.
That horizon, pink lace.
You can call me
up, try to sell
me some-
thing,
deliver a
survey.
The illusion
of eloquence is
the seat of the
judged. What dissipates
as contemporaneous

with the abscess
of human
fates. *This* lark.
That song.
The hallucinations
of trust in the
aftermath
of day peaking daily,
poking story-luck.
As if all
human relationships
turned on a
phrase. Relied
precisely on nomenclature.
You're right—variegation as a
dappled pattern of illusion
to be true. Will
love. Will never
stray apart.
These are the
articulations of brevity.

PETRA HAMMESFAHR*

Die Sünderin

She is so
coy with her
suicides.
Her temples of the
disdain-body.
If I slip
once more
out of this better
part *hallowed*
thy name,
the shell depleted of all
relevance. A
suicide slips onto
shoulders,
made inspissate:
hook-
nail-line-sinker-throat-caw-treatise.
Just to write a line, merely
to write a line.

---

* German writer of psychological fiction, often likened to Patricia Highsmith.

Then close the book

to open some

lost cover.

FRIEDRICH DÜRRENMATT*

Der Richter und sein Henker

Tremendous

appetite: mostly

remembered.

The detective spins

the knitting of

his scene.

Whole

platters of cold

cuts, a copse

of boiled

eggs. When I walk against the border

of the field, the wind is more

raucous than when I step

through the sojourn

gate. No the wind *isn't*

going to be tamed.

Bärlach's

eyes: beady.

Already

knowing the answer.

---

* Swiss writer of existential detective novels.

The field

becomes a lake

of lace. The food

previously mentioned disappears without

abbreviation

into Bärlach's

distended

stomach. Tschanz

watches him eat.

Slightly nervous.

The field isn't quiet. It is

full of mice who

decide things

about our lives.

Yes, the

green field is the premise

of guilt. Read this if you try to read this—

on a train somewhere or in your

bed. Time

passes

through the

body, which absorbs

chilled beef.

Crime passes

as well, to the guiltless,

guilty head of

Gastmann.

He may as well have done it, he has

committed impoverished

nuance. Here,

Bärlach plays the

puppeteer. I wait for you in the field in a robe made of

daisies. Oh, Bärlach knows exactly who's killed

Schmied. This is how

you will do

for me. Yes he

knows the whole time. This is what

he consumes when he

eats. Rather it is

slow Tschanz

who must stare at our

hands.

JANE EYRE

I am also
plain and little.
It is not
mild when I
thump my
wild coat, the snow
shaking from my
breast. There
is this snow
in England. I am not in
England.

A NATURAL PLAINTIFF AND DEFENDANT AT ONCE

I don't have
my own life.
The black sea
will never
come aboard me
now. I will
no more
darken to you
as the light
goes out.

SEVERAL ALARMS AND THEN AN ANSWER

The yard as
an envelope
for ash. Or
a breeze tearing
through the cat's
fur. Domesticity
isn't a crime
but there's an
open warrant
for arrest.
What you see
will disappear.
The tea things
evaporate in
steam, the
bedclothes to a
wispy cloud of
downy feathers.
Or rather, they take
place in a room
opposite a stalwart,
impenetrable

door. Door
isn't theoretical.
Nor is room,
neither *you*.
It's a way
to infuse the I
with a necessary,
voluminous
distance.
For example.
The cat rests
at *my* feet.
I love the cat—
he makes me
real. The cat
isn't a falsehood.
But he's a
temporary
placeholder in a
yard full of
light, greenery,
bees collecting
nectar for honey
as if nothing
were amiss.

They make a
home. I try
to do the same.
My apron is
burning.

WAITING FOR THE LIGHT TO CHANGE

'Lay down,'
I say. 'The wind is our
cover.' As we drive home
from the harbor.
But this morning,
sun hung like
a salt-
lick and we
were deer. So there
was a way
to *lay*
down without
strength or timidity.
All morning
yesterday,
measuring bran
for muffins.
Very tethered
to the body.
I was quantity.
Was a parcel, eking
out measurement.

Lay down to take
cover the war
says to the principals.
None of whom
are really
acting. The world
isn't a bright
document, they seem
to say. The world
is not this
usual territory.

WE COULD DECIDE TO BE ELSEWHERE

Fuck angels.

Fuck weeping angels.

AN INTERCESSION ON OBLIGATION'S BEHALF

I had expected
irony but received

a slap. All
history
recoiled.

THE SEA AS BOTH BITTER AND EXHILARATING

I am never

not a traveler

of water.

FLECKS OF LIGHT IN THIS SELF-HAVEN REVEAL A LARGER GOOD

We must be

purple careful

from now

on. Like a

djinn in desert

heat, who

awaits

the slow

accrual

of desire.

THE IMPRESSIONIST DRAWING FIGURES AT THE EDGE OF THE SEA

In brief,

as it is—

LIGHT IN WEIGHT

Stirring blue-
berries into the batter.

Will my life be

mine or will

I float? Levitation

is a sweetly

written letter. The berries

are frozen, stick together in clumps.

Levier,

from Old French.

For prying or

dislodging something.

Did I know

when I started

to wash the ink

from the paper?

ACKNOWLEDGMENTS

Thanks to the editors of these journals, where the following poems have appeared.

Aesthetix: Household Fires
Cutlass: Be Your Own Blue Swagger, Love Full Moons; With Eyes the Color of Nutmeg and Safety
Handsome: Der Abflug; Friedrich Dürrenmatt
Indefinite Space: A Place of Announcement and Reprieve; Today I Aired and Vacuumed the Cushions
Ink Node: Heloise, Who Soon Will Have No Ink
Jellyfish: Jane Eyre; Jane Eyre; Jane Eyre
La Petite Zine: We Could Decide to Be Elsewhere

"Der Abflug" is for Doro Habicht, Dirk Hoppe, Philip von Zastrow, and Stefan Weishaupt.
"A Human Saying into the Scene to Admonish Silence" is in memory of my grandfather, George C. Drai.
"But She Was Purple Calla Lily, Magnolia in Bloom" is in memory of my grandmother, Lucille Sampson Drai.
"With Eyes the Color of Nutmeg and Safety" is for Steven Meredith, my shipmate on this weird journey we call life.
"Friedrich Dürrenmatt" is for Doro Habicht and Dirk Hoppe, without whom I would never have known about the existence of 'existential detective novels.'
"The Impressionist Drawing Figures At The Edge Of The Sea" is for my uncle, Jerre Collins, with thanks for the tip.

The italicized lines in German in "Enough I Say, Relying on Marrow, Lymph, Bone" are from Paul Celan's poem, "Nachtstrahl."

The italicized lines in English are my translations of lines from the same poem. I used the line, "The track suits of modern refugees," in a poem in my chapbook, : *Body Wolf*: (Horse Less Press.)

The poem "First Lines" riffs off the first lines of various books, including works by Tolstoy, George Eliot, Marcus Aurelius, the Gospel of John, and Ralph Ellison.

Many thanks to Jamalieh Haley and Joseph Lease for readership and encouragement offered along the way. And last but not at all least, thanks to all at Black Lawrence Press, where I have been lucky enough to have found a home.

Photo: Steven Meredith

Jenny Drai is the author of *[the door]* (Trembling Pillow Press), *The New Sorrow Is Less Than The Old Sorrow* (Black Lawrence Press), and *:Body Wolf:* (Horse Less Press). Her novella, *Letters to Quince,* was awarded the Deerbird Novella Prize from Artistically Declined Press. She has worked every odd job imaginable and lived all over the place in the US and Germany. She currently resides in Bonn, where she is at work on a novel.